KW-361-763

Spreading the word
Reaching out to new learners

Spreading
the word
Reaching out to
new learners

Veronica McGivney

Published by the National Institute of
Adult Continuing Education (England and Wales)

21 De Montfort Street
Leicester LE1 7GE
Company registration no. 2603322
Charity registration no. 1002775

First published 2002

© 2002 National Institute of Adult Continuing Education (England and Wales)

All rights reserved. No reproduction, copy or transmission of this publication
may be made without the written permission of the publishers, save in
accordance with the provisions of the Copyright, Designs and Patents Act 1988,
or under the terms of any licence permitting limited copying issue by the
Copyright Licensing Agency.

The *NIACE lifelines in adult learning series* is supported by the Adult
and Community Learning Fund. ACLF is funded by the Department
for Education and Skills and managed in partnership by NIACE and
the Basic Skills Agency to develop widening participation in adult learning.

niace
promoting adult learning

NIACE has a broad remit to promote lifelong learning
opportunities for adults. NIACE works to develop
increased participation in education and training,
particularly for those who do not have easy access
because of barriers of class, gender, age, race,
language and culture, learning difficulties and
disabilities, or insufficient financial resources.

www.niace.org.uk

Cataloguing in Publication Data
A CIP record of this title is available from the British Library

Designed and typeset by Boldface
Printed in Great Britain by Russell Press, Nottingham

ISBN 1 86201 140 0

Contents

Note to the reader:
Inspirations: refer to case studies and examples of good practice.
Glossary: the meanings of the words underlined in the text can be found in the glossary on pages 40 and 41.

NIACE

1 Learning is for everyone

Surveys of adult participation in post-16 education and training programmes have consistently found that it is mostly certain groups in the population – younger adults who are employed, have some qualifications, and who are in the higher socio-economic groups – who engage in organised learning opportunities. Many of those who do not participate believe that dedicated education centres and institutions will be like school and dominated by other social groups or much younger people. In order to allay these fears and attract a wider mix of the population, education and training providers need to work outside formal institutional frameworks, contacting groups in their own communities and providing learning activities and programmes that remove the multiple barriers to access that many people experience and that are relevant to their interests and priorities. Research indicates that formerly non-participant or resistant groups and individuals often embark on planned learning pathways as a result of providers consulting them in their local areas, identifying their interests, negotiating options and customising provision.

Activities which are conducted outside a provider's main buildings or campuses are often labelled 'outreach'. They are necessary for a number of reasons:

- to raise awareness of available learning opportunities among the groups who traditionally do not participate in organised learning;
- to identify communities or groups who have not been reached and who may have unmet learning interests and needs;
- to take learning opportunities to groups and individuals who are unable to access provision for reasons such as family responsibilities, difficulties with costs and transport, age, disability or poor health and to those who are resistant because of former educational experiences, fear or apprehension;
- to develop new methods of educational delivery that overcome problems related to time, distance and mobility;
- to develop new learning programmes that respond to expressed interests and needs;
- to meet Government or funding requirements to increase overall numbers of students or those from particular postcode areas.

2 The evidence

There is widespread recognition among adult education researchers, analysts and practitioners that outreach work is one of the most effective ways of attracting new and different learners, especially those who are most <u>socially excluded</u>.

> **There's no substitute for talking to people (Outreach worker)**

> **Outreach and development work is often the vital prelude to eventually wider participation. The precise outcomes may be difficult to calibrate but the general benefits are not at all to be doubted.**
>
> **In inner-city areas only very local centres can help make education accessible to individuals and communities otherwise excluded by distance, transport or cultural barriers.**
> (The Fryer report, *Learning for the 21st Century* (1997))

> **The important thing is the first hook. Once you've got them through the door the possibilities are endless. It's the investment in that stage which is the most important.**
> (Community education worker)

You've got to spend time on the pre-figurative stuff in the community; talking to people. But no-one sees this as real work. It's too loose and unstructured, but you can't reach these people any other way. (Outreach worker)

You could say the battle's won once you've got them through the door. It's the previous nine months that are the really hard work. Outreach work needs to be done in the pub and that often means in the evening. You need staff and resources to do this. (Community education worker)

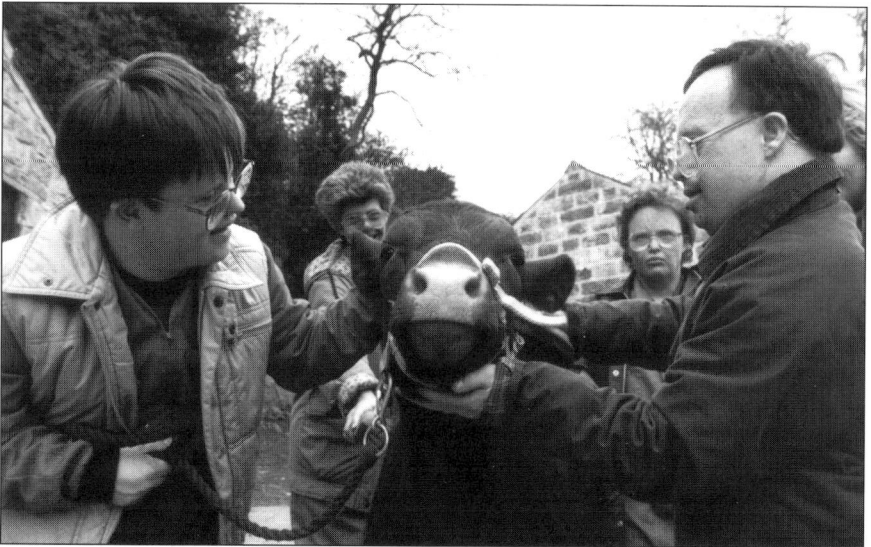

NICK HAYES

3 A favourable political climate

Working locally with excluded groups and communities is a key dimension of the Government's anti-poverty, community regeneration and lifelong learning strategies. Adult and community learning is expected to play a critical role in the neighbourhood renewal strategy.

In the Green Paper *The Learning Age* (DfEE, 1998) outreach programmes for adults were described as making a 'valuable contribution to lifelong learning' and further and higher education funding councils and institutions were recommended to attach 'high priority' to their continuation.

The Adult and Community Learning Fund (ACLF) was created by the new Labour Government specifically to support:

activities that will take learning into new sectors of the community not reached by traditional education organisations, providing opportunities that are relevant to the people involved and delivering them in ways that will interest and attract the people who are hardest to reach.
(*ACLF Prospectus*, DfEE, 1998)

The importance and desirability of outreach working has also been a recurrent theme in the reports of a number of enquiries commissioned by the Government. In its influential final report, for example, the Policy Action Team on Skills stressed the importance to community renewal of locally-based, locally-inspired learning activities.

"[They should be] delivered where people live through neighbourhood learning centres in the management and operation of which local people should, wherever possible, have a significant stake. [These] could take a variety of forms, including FE premises used for outreach work, Lifelong Learning centres as well as local community centres."
(*Skills for neighbourhood renewal: local solutions*, the report of the Policy Action Team on Skills, DfEE, 1999)

The report noted that in the disadvantaged areas studied by the Action Team, there was often 'a disturbing lack of connection between educational institutions and some of the local communities they exist to serve'. It found that first-rung provision of the kind most likely to appeal to groups sceptical or hesitant about the value of learning was insufficiently available:

in part because public policy has concentrated strongly in recent years on providing education and training leading to qualifications. This has led to a significant mismatch between the provision that is available and what is actually needed.

"Much more of the right kind of learning will be available in ways that meet the needs of local people, on their own terms and in settings with which they are comfortable. (…) Local learning opportunities, where people learn together in locally-based, familiar environments, provide the key link to learning for individuals of all ages." (*Learning and Skills Council Prospectus*, DfEE, 1999)

"[Local authorities will] offer innovative ways of ensuring that learning is fully integrated into economic, social and regeneration strategies, the development of community capacity and the renewal of civic engagement." (*Learning and Skills Council Prospectus*, DfEE, 1999)

In the light of these findings and similar evidence from other national commissions and enquiries, the former Secretary of State for Education and Employment, David Blunkett, put a strong emphasis on the development of locally-based, non-accredited learning provision as a means of achieving wider participation in learning. He also demanded that 65 per cent of additional adult learners should be drawn from groups whose background had disadvantaged them. Reaching out to new and different adult learners has therefore become an important part of post-16 education policy and has been written into the remit of the Learning and Skills Council (LSC).

The *LSC Prospectus* also gave local authorities a much stronger community role than they have had in the recent past.

In the last few years Local Strategic Partnerships, many operating within local authority boundaries, have been set up. These are intended to bring education providers and the communities they serve together in implementing neighbourhood renewal and working collaboratively to bring about change.

Outreach has therefore recovered its key role in local learning strategies.

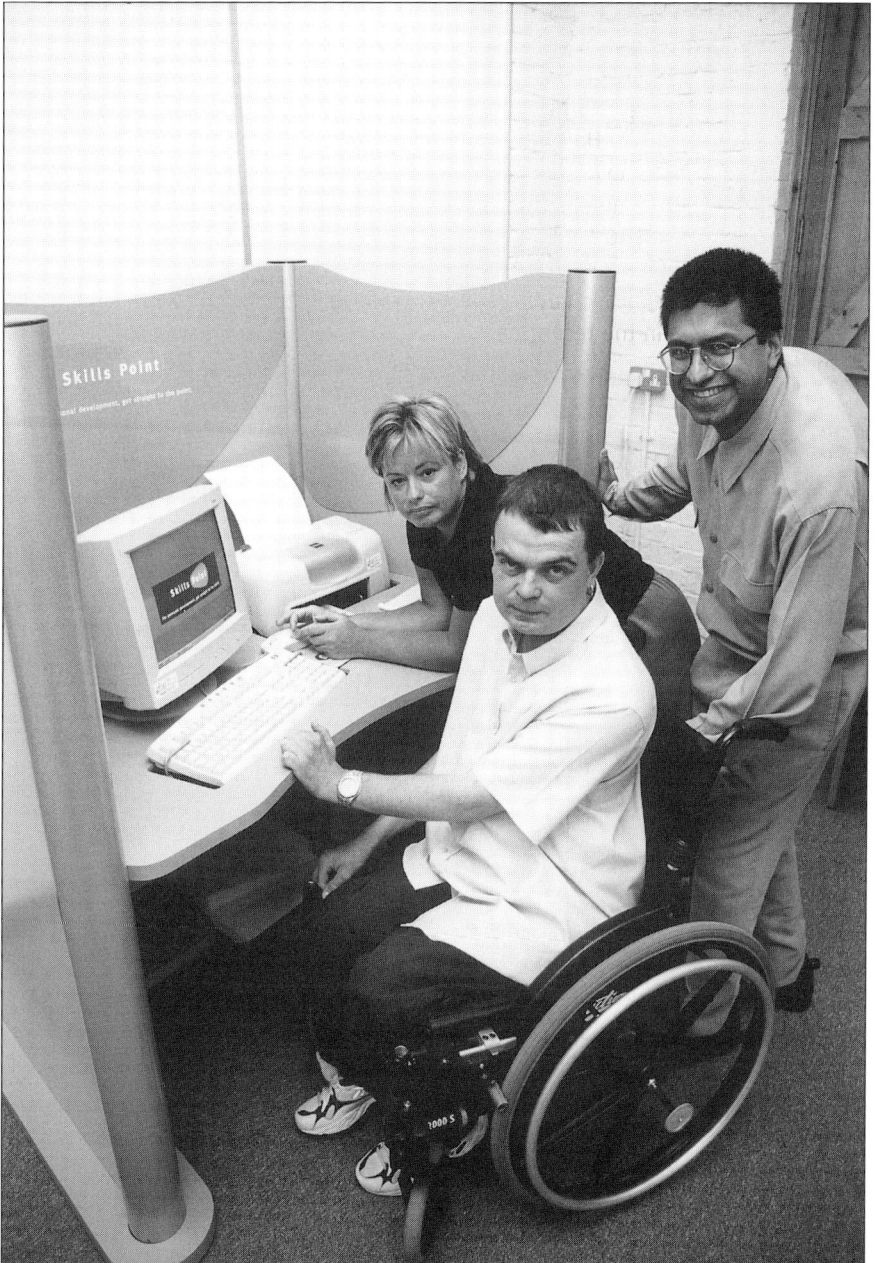

4 Understandings of 'outreach'

There is no single, universally accepted definition of 'outreach'. It has become an imprecise, catch-all term that tends to be applied to any activity that goes on outside the main premises of an education institution or organisation. While the central connotation is to work outside a main centre or institution (a staff activity), the term has acquired a number of other meanings:

- engaging groups identified as economically, socially and educationally disadvantaged in learning (widening participation);
- raising awareness of existing learning opportunities and educational services (a marketing or recruitment strategy);
- mounting learning programmes in community locations (a delivery mechanism);
- liaising and making contact with community organisations and groups (a networking process);
- working in informal and participative ways with people outside a centre or institution (a method or an approach);
- developing new learning programmes in response to identified needs (curriculum development);
- providing community-based learning activities as a stepping stone to mainstream programmes (building progression routes);
- training local people as animateurs, signposters, learning champions or community change agents (capacity-building);
- assisting community groups in developing their own activities (a community support process).

The most widely accepted understanding of educational outreach is as a two-pronged process that involves: 1) increasing local communities' awareness of available learning opportunities; and 2) using local venues for extending mainstream courses into the community and/or developing new programmes in response to identified demand and needs.

Outreach is also now widely perceived as a process designed to draw into learning the most socially, economically and educationally disadvantaged. In the last few years, the term has been used synonymously with others such as social inclusion and widening participation which also imply a reaching-out to excluded sections of the community.

The different understandings of outreach reflect differing views about the nature and aims of this kind of work. Some providers see it mainly as a marketing tool to increase the number of participants in existing provision (this is a top-down, supply-side approach in which the interests of the provider are paramount). Others view it as a means of giving people opportunities to negotiate, plan and control the kinds of learning activities they engage in (a demand-led approach in which the interests of learners are paramount). In the latter case, outreach is construed as a process of consultation and consensus leading to joint planning of activities and programmes that respond to people's expressed interests. This approach empowers people as stakeholders in their own learning:

> Outreach is a process whereby people who would not normally use adult education are contacted in non-institutional settings and become involved in attending and eventually in jointly planning and controlling activities, schemes and courses relevant to their circumstances and needs.
> (Kevin Ward, *Replan Review* 1, 1986)

MICHAEL STOCKTON

5 Models and approaches

Educational outreach activities can take a number of different forms. Some of these fall into categories that have been defined in youth work:

- The satellite model (establishing outreach centres for delivering learning programmes in community locations);
- The peripatetic model (delivering learning programmes in organisational settings such as hostels, day centres, homes for the elderly, community centres, hospitals, prisons);
- The detached outreach model (contacting people outside agency or organisational settings, for example in streets, shopping centres, pubs, at school gates);
- The domiciliary outreach model (visiting people in their own homes).

The first three approaches are commonly used in educational outreach strategies. For example, many post-16 providers serving large, diverse and far-flung populations deliver learning programmes in specially-established community locations. Others use existing social meeting places such as pubs and clubs for the delivery of outreach programmes. The domiciliary model is often used in work with people with disabilities and, sometimes, those with literacy needs.

An increasingly popular outreach approach is the use of mobile services, stocked with laptops and literature on education and training opportunities, which provide drop-in information and guidance and help with literacy, numeracy and computer skills in locations such as shopping centres, car parks, outlying estates and rural areas. Access buses, which travel around local communities encouraging people to engage in learning, have been used in places such as Wales, Lancashire, Liverpool, Derbyshire and the North West.

Other increasingly common outreach approaches are distance learning strategies (such as IT learning networks for people in rural locations) and local capacity-building programmes (training local people as guidance workers, local learning ambassadors or learning champions).

ASPIRATIONS

Knowsley Community College

Knowsley Community College has 123 LINC centres (Learning in Neighbourhood Centres) located in primary schools, youth clubs, libraries, community centres, blocks of flats and other community venues.

University of Sussex

The University of Sussex runs learning programmes in a flat in a deprived estate in Hastings.

Local authority outreach

Many local authorities deliver information, guidance and learning programmes in community venues such as schools, community centres, residential homes and isolated estates. Some have established 'learning shops' in main streets or libraries. Others have established 'community learning zones' or developed community-based ICT (Information and Communications Technology) approaches for certain groups. Some (for example Oxfordshire) have developed a strong authority- or country-wide outreach strategy as part of their lifelong learning plan.

Bolton Information Network

A scheme linked to the Bolton Information Network has trained local people in outreach work, communication skills, advice and guidance, working with others and basic skills awareness. The resulting team of community learning ambassadors attracts different groups into learning, supports learners and helps them to progress in a number of ways.

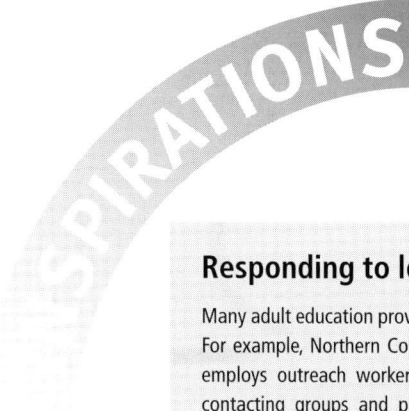

Responding to local learning needs

Many adult education providers traditionally employ an outreach approach. For example, Northern College, an adult residential college near Barnsley, employs outreach workers who work in neighbouring local authorities contacting groups and providing bespoke courses in response to their expressed interests and demands.

Much of WEA (Workers' Educational Association) work is also conducted on an outreach basis:

Education is taken out to the learners. Local communities are supported and encouraged to become involved in the administration of projects and gradually to take responsibility for their own learning (…). The WEA sees genuinely student-centred approaches as critical to the inclusion and engagement of many more individuals and communities in lifelong learning.

(Ford, G, and Jackson, H (1999) *The WEA and Partnerships*, WEA National Association, London)

NICK HAYES

6 Embarking on an outreach strategy

In order to conduct outreach work effectively, the three essential factors are:

● Managerial support and commitment
● Adequate resourcing
● The right staff with the right skills.

Managerial support

Undertaking outreach involves important prior decisions about levels of resourcing and coverage. The full commitment and support of managers is therefore critical. This should involve:

● recognising that outreach is an integral part of an institution's work, not auto-matically low-level or second best;
● setting realistic and achievable aims and targets;
● recognising that effective work in the community requires time and flexibility and allowing for this in work schedules;
● discussing with outreach workers how to make the most effective response to identified interests and needs;
● providing workers with adequate supervision and mechanisms for regular analysis and evaluation of the work;
● providing support to help workers address the kind of problems that arise in outreach work;
● ensuring that institution-based staff understand the role of outreach workers and that outreach staff are integrated with and see themselves as part of the whole-staff team rather than being on the margins;
● providing adequate infrastructure support (office accommodation, administra-tive and clerical support, telephone).

Oxfordshire County Council

Oxfordshire County Council has a county-wide outreach team which covers the county, with each worker having a particular patch to work in. All workers are offered accredited training. Outreach is seen as an integral part of the service and there has been a deliberate attempt to reduce worker isolation. Each member of the team is based in an Adult Education Centre where they can relate directly to colleagues. There are regular team meetings as well as meetings with staff working in areas such as guidance, literacy and numeracy and learning difficulties.

University of Sussex

The University of Sussex has used Higher Education Funding Council and European funding, together with smaller pockets of funding from the Arts Council and health trusts, to provide learning activities, educational guidance and support for people living in peripheral housing estates outside Brighton, Hastings and Crawley.

Resources

The effectiveness of outreach activity also depends on the resources made available for it. A number of different sources of finance – the Single Regeneration Budget (SRB), the Adult and Community Learning Fund (ACLF), Non-Schedule 2 pilots, the Lottery (New Opportunities Fund), the Community Development Learning Fund, Education Action Zone funds and the European Social Fund – have been used to support outreach strategies that widen participation and encourage community regeneration. The 47 Local Learning and Skills Councils also have discretionary funds available for adult and community learning, guidance, widening participation and local regeneration initiatives. These funding sources are generally considered more flexible than mainstream formula funding as they enable innovation. However, they are short-term and have to be bid for. Many providers use a cocktail of different funding streams to support their outreach activities.

Ideally, outreach should be supported by both short-term and more permanent funding – the first to permit experimentation and innovation; the second to allow providers to establish a sustained presence in communities and have a long-term impact.

However, there can be conflict between outreach work designed to further the development of different communities and the audit culture operated by mainstream funding regimes. Most formula funding rewards education providers more for student recruitment and individual educational progression than for helping communities to embark on a process of positive change, although the latter is one of the best ways of bringing about neighbourhood renewal.

The right staff

The third essential prerequisite for successful outreach is finding workers with the right attributes and blend of skills. These may have less to do with qualifications than with personal characteristics such as good communication and listening skills. For the effectiveness of any outreach endeavour depends ultimately on the web of relationships which workers are able to establish in the community.

Those involved in contacting people who do not take advantage of organised learning opportunities are more likely to be accepted when they have backgrounds and characteristics similar to those of the target groups. People of the same gender and ethnic group, who speak the same language (or with the same accent), and who have local credibility, are more likely to be trusted than those who do not have any characteristics in common with the targeted groups.

Skill needs

Outreach workers have to accomplish a number of complex tasks which require a range of practical and interpersonal skills. At the initial stage they may need to:

- conduct local research and analyse the resulting data;
- identify key local networks and individuals;
- contact and negotiate with a range of different agencies, groups and individuals and deal with people at both official and grassroots level;
- develop partnerships with local agencies and other providers;
- organise and administer meetings with disparate groups and agencies;
- engage people, as individuals or in groups, in dialogue about their interests and priorities;
- offer information, advice and guidance on available opportunities and resources;
- identify learning interests and needs and devise appropriate ways of meeting them;
- broker provision between groups and providers;
- locate and negotiate use of premises.

At the programme delivery stage, outreach workers need the ability to:

- organise and administer programmes in response to identified interests;
- help groups to identify programme aims and objectives without imposing their own preferences and values;
- facilitate activities (without controlling them);
- help people to identify their existing knowledge skills and talents;
- establish mechanisms for progression routes and referrals to other providers, resource agencies or information sources;
- find resources to provide any forms of support that are required (such as transport, costs, child-care, support for people with disabilities);
- evaluate progress and outcomes;
- monitor and evaluate the work and produce written reports.

In performing these and other tasks, outreach workers need to have sensitivity; respect for others and the host communities; the ability to listen and convert what they hear into constructive activity; the ability to adapt to different groups and different situations and to react to widely-differing wants and needs.

They also need to work autonomously, sometimes in isolation, and handle conflict.

Not everyone has the right personality and combination of skills to do outreach work and staff development is essential not only for outreach workers themselves but also for tutors who are not used to working in non-institutional settings or working with non-traditional learners. Staff development programmes would also help managers and institution-based staff to benefit from the knowledge and the expertise of outreach staff in supporting the mainstream participation and progression of new learner groups.

Effective community-based provision demands a range of skills on the part of providers. These include negotiation, facilitation, appropriate teaching and learning styles, guidance, networking, development planning and financial management. While some practitioners have developed expertise in many of these areas, others have had minimal support. All staff engaged in such provision need to upgrade their skills and to learn from the expertise of colleagues from other sectors (Scottish Office, 1996)

7 Implementing an outreach strategy

Outreach work can be divided into a number of stages:

- an audit of the provider's existing learner profile;
- identification of missing groups;
- identification of possible target areas, communities and groups;
- conducting research into the target areas or communities;
- establishing relationships with agencies and individuals working in the same areas and with the same groups;
- making contact with people in the target groups and engaging them in a process of identifying their learning interests and needs;
- negotiating learning activities with the target groups;
- working with the provider to deliver the learning programmes agreed with groups;
- supporting learners through the learning process.

Targeting

Few providers have sufficient resources or staff available to work across their whole catchment area and some targeting will be necessary.

Providers may wish to target specific locations (for example, housing estates) or particular communities (ethnic groups, lone parents, refugees, travellers, older adults, unemployed men). They may also want to provide programmes for groups whose circumstances prohibit attending a centre or institution (the elderly, the homebound, people with disabilities, people in residential centres or bail hostels).

Other providers may already have a tradition of working with certain groups such as people with profound and multiple learning difficulties.

In deciding where and at whom to target outreach efforts, difficult choices may have to be made. Any area or segment of the population may contain a plethora of different groups, each with different and perhaps competing interests and priorities. Local sensitivities must be taken into account. If outreach workers are seen to be too associated with a particular group or community they may become the object of resentment or suspicion to others.

Networking and collaboration

The establishment of inter-agency partnerships and co-operative networks is critical in outreach work and vital to its effectiveness. In order to reach some groups it will be necessary to engage in preliminary dialogue with the range of agencies, organisations and individuals already in contact and working with them. These might include:

- Other mainstream and community education providers;
- Guidance services;
- Local schools and pre-school nurseries or play groups;
- Voluntary organisations;
- Community groups;
- Housing and tenants associations;
- Social services, health and welfare professionals and organisations;
- Local religious organisations;
- Employers;
- Probation officers.

It is very important to establish a relationship of trust and co-operation with such agencies both to reach the target groups and to reassure them that the service is intended to complement – not compete with – their work.

> For outreach to be effective means developing a relationship with other organisations, community groups and communities that can be sustained over a long period of time. A lot of the successful work we've done is only because of the sustained nature of our relationship within the community over a long period. (HE project officer)

Some common pitfalls

Territorial problems are probably inevitable in outreach work:

One AE organiser told the worker, 'You are treading on my toes'. A local worker for a national charity operating a community-based resource centre in a severely deprived area refused the college its crèche facility for outreach purposes commenting, 'I don't see any reason for the voluntary sector to underwrite the statutory sector.'

These comments tended to reflect a wider sense of unease within some sections of community-based groups, especially in the early stages of the project.

(Kinneavy, T (1989) *The Outreach College: design and implementation*, FEU/REPLAN)

Some outreach projects have experienced problems arising from multiple use of premises. Lack of co-operation and rivalries between different services using the same venues is a common situation. To deal with issues such as these requires considerable tact and diplomacy.

It is an important principle in outreach work [to] establish co-operative links with other providers of services who are working in the same geographic area. Many providers have long histories of educational involvement in local communities which may be formally established, as with AE and the WEA, or informally organised by voluntary associations, who nevertheless contribute equally to local AE activities. (…) Contact and communication between the college and the various other providers becomes important if suspicion and distrust are to be overcome and fears of territorial encroachment are to be allayed. (Kinneavy, T (1989) *The Outreach College: design and implementation*, FEU/REPLAN)

SPIRATIONS

South Trafford College

South Trafford College has worked with tenants on an estate to help them manage the transfer of council housing to housing association tenure which would involve them in the running of estates. This entailed working in partnership with tenants' associations, a credit union, a church, various community groups, a local school, the Housing Department, the Housing Association, the Credit Union, the Youth Service and Trafford Council.

Royal Forest of Dean College

An outreach guidance worker based at Royal Forest of Dean College networks with a wide range of rural groups and agencies including family centres, Opportunity Centres (for disabled children and those with learning difficulties and their families), Gloucester Mental Health Association, Women's Refuge, a centre for the unemployed and an information shop for young people.

Park Lane College

Park Lane College in Leeds provides learning opportunities at a large number of sites dispersed around the city. The community-based work involves contact and networking with a large number of other organisations and services including schools, Family Service Units, the Education Support Agency, the Probation Service, the Youth Service, NHS trusts, voluntary organisations, Leeds Play Network, local employment and training services, Mental Health Advocacy and health groups.

Bristol Community Education Service

The Community Education Service in Bristol works with local community organisations and activists on a wide range of community development projects and programmes. The service provides funding to self-organised community groups who have been successful at designing and running their own community development learning programmes.

8 Making the right contacts

Reaching and contacting target groups is the central activity involved in outreach. Most outreach workers operate through a mixture of 'cold' contacts – door-knocking, handing out leaflets, approaching people in the street, at school gates, and so on – and 'snowballing' contacts: following up leads and contacts provided by others. However, it is important to identify the right 'others'. To establish the most appropriate contacts involves time and considerable skill and, in some cases, contact with groups can only be achieved through a specific intermediary.

In order to familiarise themselves with different areas and communities, outreach workers need to identify the main communication channels and 'key' local people and opinion leaders – those with a high profile who are known and respected in a neighbourhood and familiar with local issues. This involves spending time in an area, observing, interacting with and listening to local residents in order to get a feel for the local networks.

Working with organisations or people who already have a high profile and positive image helps to establish credibility and reduces lead-time. Local knowledge can also help workers to avoid mistakes. The 'chemistry' of local areas varies greatly. In each area there will be different organisations, institutions and community leaders/ activists involved in community matters and it is possible for workers to follow false trails by cultivating the wrong people or inappropriate groups.

The secret lies in identifying individuals, groups and organisations:

- who have the capacity to communicate with a wide range of other people and organisations through whom local energy is effectively channelled;
- who have the ability to develop and maintain adequate arrangements for the support and nurturing of collective effort;
- who are well-regarded by the target audience and organisations with which you are particularly concerned.

(FEU/REPLAN (1990) *Drawing on Experience*, REPLAN Projects Review)

Working with the gatekeepers

Negotiating with community leaders and other gatekeepers is one of the most important aspects of outreach as the success of any outreach initiative depends on their co-operation, commitment and support. Gaining these depends on the extent to which they can be persuaded of the value of the work both to the target groups and to themselves. Some outreach and development workers have found that gaining the co-operation of the gatekeepers is far more difficult than persuading the target groups to engage in learning.

To mediate with gatekeepers (such as employers, religious leaders, wardens, community group leaders), outreach workers need considerable tact, persistence and persuasiveness. They need to enter into an early dialogue with them about the nature and purposes of the educational activities proposed and their potential outcomes. Getting the messages right at this stage is crucial for, in order to give their support, these individuals must be persuaded that they have more to gain than to lose. Like any other group the gatekeepers have diverse characteristics, values, pressures and priorities and approaches to them need to be just as sensitive as approaches to the groups providers are trying to reach.

Consulting the target groups

Institutional outreach is sometimes conducted more with the aim of raising awareness of mainstream services than with a view to responding to new needs.

Although there may be token dialogue, this often consists simply of asking people to state their learning preferences rather than engaging them in discussions about their experience and concerns. The consultation process should not just be a matter of asking people what they want to learn, but an in-depth dialogue which allows interests, needs and priorities to emerge in a way that might not happen if they are simply were presented with a traditional, pre-packaged adult education 'menu' to choose from.

Responding to emerging learning interests and needs

The community consultation process has important implications for the providing organisation. When new learning needs are identified through the consultation process, outreach workers need to be able to address them promptly in order to maintain community credibility. The ultimate test of the effectiveness of any outreach activity is whether emerging learning interests are translated into practical service delivery.

Selection of outreach venues

The importance of using familiar, non-threatening settings for learning delivery cannot be under-estimated. The location of learning can be as important as its focus. This is due not only to practical but also to psychological and cultural factors. In some deprived areas, many people are reluctant to go beyond their familiar local boundaries.

It goes without saying that the locations chosen for delivery of local learning activities should be venues in which learners feel safe and comfortable and which are attractive, welcoming and open at times that suit learners.

Connections with mainstream

Outreach activities and provision should be linked to an organisation's mainstream work. Outreach will be of limited value if it is a single, one-off, out-based exercise conducted without connection to the main work of a provider. If outreach strategies are totally disconnected from mainstream, they are likely to remain marginal.

The process of connecting with new and different learners should produce some changes in institutional culture and practices. If it does not, learners who move from community-based into mainstream learning may fail to achieve and withdraw from programmes.

> If learning interests are identified you've got to do it now. There's no point in saying something will be starting in September.
> (Community education worker)

> You have to have programmes running at all times so that people can start at any time. When they trickle in, you need to give them something that day, not next September.
> (College outreach worker)

Residential care home staff in Oxford

An outreach worker in Oxford wishing to work with low-qualified staff in residential care homes sent an initial letter to owners and managers of 20 homes. The letter explained the scheme and emphasised the value of raising workers' education and skill levels. It also invited owners and managers to take part in short telephone interviews to assess the skill needs required in the homes and the training needs of care workers. The letter was followed up by telephone contacts to arrange the interviews. After the interviews employers were invited to send one or two of their workers without qualifications onto an accredited course. A number needed persuading that there would be no disadvantages to them by sending workers on the scheme.

Guidance provision in doctors' surgeries

In Gloucester and Nottingham, educational guidance has been provided in doctors' surgeries. This has enabled many people to talk about their learning interests and constraints in a familiar setting in which they feel comfortable.

9 Assessing the impact of outreach

How do you know whether outreach work has made a difference? Assessing the impact of outreach activities can be very difficult because they are by their very nature very diverse.
In addition,

- outreach activities are often conducted with groups who are hard to reach and who may need time to develop trust and confidence before they engage in organised learning;
- outreach activities are often innovative and experimental and tangible outcomes may not evident for some time;
- for some disadvantaged groups it would be unrealistic to expect immediate outcomes in the form of movement to progressively more advanced levels of learning.

It can therefore be extremely difficult to measure or quantify the outcomes of outreach work. Some kinds of outreach activity do not directly generate student numbers. It is impossible, for example, to discover precisely what action has been taken in response to outreach activities such as publicity and guidance, and how

> You're only scratching the surface in three years in trying to change these communities.
> (Community development worker)

> People here are hugely lacking in confidence. They often have no hope of being or doing anything.
> (Outreach worker)

valuable local contacts and networks are. While it may be possible to count the number of people contacted and services provided, it is far more difficult to measure the effect of those services on the attitudes, motivations and behaviour of targeted individuals and groups. Changes in attitudes and feelings are both difficult to quantify and difficult to attribute to specific events and circumstances.

Nevertheless, some evaluation strategies should be built into the design of outreach activities from the start in order to ensure that the original aims are achieved, to try and monitor the impact of interventions and, where necessary, to improve their effectiveness.

Outreach should be evaluated for its impact both on the communities and individuals concerned and on the providing institution. Evaluation strategies might include investment in good management information systems, follow-up of samples of the people contacted and focus groups with those who have engaged in learning activity. Where possible, target groups should be involved in evaluating the effectiveness of outreach programmes themselves. Many providers are worried about proving that outreach is 'value for money'. Because of the diversity of outreach activities and the range of possible outcomes, there can be no single method of calculating costs and benefits and some find that it is easier to evaluate on a case-by-case basis.

The results of outreach are not always those that are expected. Although outreach work does not always result in individual progression to mainstream learning programmes, the results for individuals, families and communities can be profound.

> **A lot of local schools say that their Ofsted reports have been much better than expected. There are positive spin-offs from parents learning (...). In a place like this where there are appalling GCSE rates, we need as many positive role models as possible. If you've got mum, auntie, brother or sister in education and training, the impact is incalculable. If we didn't believe that we would have chopped it [outreach work] years ago because if you only take [educational] progression into account you'd obviously be making a loss.** (College manager)

Carrwood Centre, Bradford

The Carrwood Centre in Bradford has provided short initiatives for residents on local estates, mainly families of white origin from socially disadvantaged backgrounds. Courses were all relevant to the needs of local people and included 'Get Crafty', providing the opportunity to learn and develop skills in decorating, painting, curtain-making and restoring dilapidated furniture; Community Sports Leadership Training; Working with Citizens and Positive Parenting. 'The courses have given many people a new focus and direction in their lives, as well as enabling them to positively contribute to their community. The local school has benefited from the students running two sports clubs for the children during the lunch break and after school.'

(Aldridge, F (1999) *Short and Sweet*, Leicester: NIACE)

Clayton Brook Community Learning Project

The Clayton Brook Community Learning Project recently acquired a Community House on the estate. Two workshops were facilitated on special paint effects and soft furnishings, the objective being to teach local volunteers new skills which would enable them to participate in the refurbishment of the Community House, as well as learning new ideas for their own homes. One young lady with no previous experience of sewing attended the soft furnishings workshop. Although at first somewhat hesitant and shy, she soon gained confidence as she leant new skills. By the end of the workshop she had learnt how to measure, cut out, use a sewing machine, and assemble curtains. She took a pair of curtains home to finish, proudly returning to present them to the house a few days later.

(Aldridge, F (1999), *Short and Sweet*, Leicester, NIACE.)

10 Keeping the work going

Sustainability is a real issue for outreach work that is funded on a temporary basis and this raises questions about how to manage the cessation of funding. Without a strategy for embedding it, the work that has been started will not bear dividends beyond the funding period. Some short-lived outreach activities have raised expectations that cannot be met. Continuation strategies need to be in place if initiatives are to have any lasting impact and providers are to maintain trust and credibility. Groups who feel they have been let down may not be inclined to accept other approaches from education providers in the future.

Conducting outreach activities with groups that are already established can help to sustain work beyond the funding period. If completely new groups are formed to take part in educational outreach activities, the chances are that they will disperse when those activities come to an end. If the work is undertaken with an established group there is a better chance of its being taken forward and contributing to subsequent activities:

> 'The best practice is where education provision builds on other community
> activity such as tenants' issues, with tutors in a facilitating role.'
> (WEA worker)

Some outreach workers have circumvented the problem of short-term funding by finding other sources of financial support. However, there may be pitfalls in moving to a less flexible funding regime as it could impose changes on the nature and style of the work.

Training local people to take the work on

Outreach workers cannot work exclusively in the same area or with the same groups of people. At some point they may have to leave, although withdrawal should be gradual rather than abrupt.

An increasingly popular dimension of educational outreach is therefore the recruitment of local people who have local contacts and credibility within different communities, and training them to be learning champions, ambassadors or guidance 'signposters' who can take the work further when projects come to an end.

Training local workers has been a feature of some recent outreach projects. It has entailed on-the-job training as well as participation in accredited training programmes and referral to other projects providing training. Those implementing such a strategy should ensure, however, that the people involved do not endanger, or lose, their entitlement to benefits.

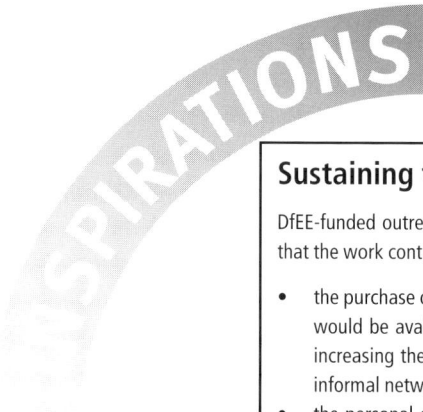

Sustaining the outreach work

DfEE-funded outreach projects used a range of strategies for ensuring that the work continued in some form. These included:

- the purchase or sharing of computer-aided guidance packages that would be available to the community beyond the funding period, increasing the feeling of community on an estate, and developing informal networks amongst residents;
- the personal development of volunteers, including the facilitation of support groups;
- building up links with schools and agreeing to work collaboratively to provide literacy classes for parents;
- establishing formal networks of contacts for community workers which raise morale and provide a framework for lobbying, information-giving and acting as an intermediary to LEA provision.

One project sought to build sustainability for the future by adopting a cascade model. Each volunteer was encouraged to run three presentations for their family, friends, neighbours and other contacts. Most of the attendees were non-learners for whom the intended outcome was a guidance interview or learning programme. In this way, the word was intended to be spread as widely as possible, using local 'ambassadors', rather than through the 'professionals'.

Watson, A, and Tyers, C, (1998), *Demonstration Outreach Projects: identification of good practice*, Final Report, National overview with individual project reports, DfEE/ SWA Consulting

11 Check it out

Issues and challenges for providers

- Is outreach work integral to your work or a marginal extra? If the latter, it is unlikely to have much effect.
- Is it part of a coherent strategy to widen participation and improve learning opportunities for adults?
- What you are conducting outreach *for*? Is it to increase the number of learners for mainstream programmes or to help different communities define their own learning needs? Outreach may have outcomes beyond increased student recruitment and progression. If the latter are the only prized and recorded results, other broader and more valuable outcomes for individuals, families and communities may not be acknowledged.
- Have you allowed realistic time-scales for the necessary development work to take place before outputs are required? Change can be a long-term process and some time may elapse before the outcomes of informal learning may be visible. As an instrument for widening participation in learning, outreach must be seen as a long-term investment. It needs to be supported in a way that takes into account that outcomes, in terms of visible changes in attitude and behaviour, are more likely to be seen in the long- rather than short-term.
- Have you got the right workers? Success in outreach depends on investing in the people with the ability to network and gain the trust of a number of different constituencies. People engaged to do this work should not always be on short-term contracts but should enjoy terms and conditions of employment that are on a par with those of institution-based staff: 'It's not easy if you're on a temporary contract to put your heart and soul into a community and there's early burn-out because of the intensity of support that's required.' (College outreach worker)
- Outreach work and those who conduct it need the full support of senior managers. What kind of support and supervision mechanisms are available for outreach workers?
- Where and at whom do you target outreach activity? This may involve difficult choices as concentrating on particular groups and residential areas may mean that others are left out. All communities contain groups with conflicting needs and demands.

Some priority areas attract a variety of different and often unconnected regeneration funding streams. This can lead to a proliferation of unconnected interventions leading to duplication and conflicts with other agencies. It can also mean that areas with pockets of similar deprivation are neglected.

- Are your outreach programmes low level and remedial in nature? 'Outreach' has become closely associated with the concept of disadvantage and low-level work. While it is important to direct activities towards those groups identified as most socially, economically and educationally deprived, the effect can be to 'pathologise' the people concerned. If outreach is seen only or principally as a means of combating disadvantage, it may result in a blurring of the boundary between an education intervention and a social service one. It can also imply deficiencies in the people targeted.

  It is also easy to fall into the trap of imposing one's own values and preference, and using outreach as a remedial rather than transformative tool, which results in the work being automatically perceived as low level.

- How responsive are the programmes that you provide to people's own interests and needs? People are more likely to engage in learning when they are given the opportunity to decide what is of value and relevance to them than when they are offered pre-packaged education or training programmes. Provision that is customised to the interests and requirements of new learners will have a greater and more positive impact on individuals and communities than the achievement of pre-determined objectives set by providers.

- How promptly do you respond to community learning needs? When needs are identified a prompt response is essential – 'getting people when they're all fired up'. There should not be too long a gap between a local needs analysis and actually setting things up. If providers fail to act on the suggestions generated through the community consultation process, the integrity of the worker may be called into question.

- Is sufficient value placed on community-based provision? Community-based learning should not be planned with the sole aim of pushing students up an educational ladder. First steps in learning should be valued for themselves as well as a springboard to more formal learning, qualifications and employment.

- Are outreach workers offered staff development and accreditation?

- Are you using the lessons generated by successful outreach practices to inform mainstream procedures and practices? Outreach work should be seen as the *beginning* of a process of engagement with local communities, not the end. It should not be marginalised and conducted in isolation from providers' mainstream work.

Issues and challenges for outreach workers

Although outreach work can be personally very rewarding, many workers routinely experience a number of challenges. The major ones are:

- lack of institutional support;
- combating community resistance and distrust of education institutions;
- being fair (and being seen to be fair) in allocations of resources and dealings with different groups even when they have conflicting views and needs;
- the need to avoid becoming overly associated with a particular group, as this can lead to rejection by others;
- working within inflexible funding regimes;
- isolation and working entirely on one's own;
- insufficient recognition, by managers and funders, of how much time it takes before results can be seen;
- persuading managers to recognise outcomes other than increased recruitment and other benefits for the institution;
- conflicts of values when institutional values are not compatible with those of the target communities. Pre-conceived ideas about what people want or need can be deeply resented.

All of these challenges need to be anticipated and strategies for avoiding or dealing with them should be devised with the help of managers and co-workers. The following suggestions may help.

A few tips

Find yourself marginalised within your institution? Ensure that you know exactly what your role is and who in the organisation you are accountable to. Ask for a managerial champion or mentor who can support you and ensure that you are a fully integrated staff member.

Make sure that you get to know key staff members – senior managers, access and guidance staff, widening participation managers and heads of department – who may be in a position to support your work.

Request that you be invited to attend staff meetings and other cross-institutional events so that all staff can become familiar with your work, its importance and its outcomes and potential outcomes, both for the groups concerned and for the organisation. Make sure from the start that you will have access to adequate clerical and administrative support.

Can't find the right contacts? Observe people in their groups for a while. Who is the person that others listen to in the pub, at the school gates, at the Parent and Toddler or pre-school group? Identifying and gaining the trust of opinion leaders within different groups is often more useful than consulting professionals working in an area. Other people in the group often follow their lead.

Having difficulty persuading the 'gatekeepers'? Think of all the ways in which the proposed activities might benefit them as well as the people they are in contact with, and if possible offer them some sweeteners (one outreach worker arranged for part-time workers in care homes to be replaced, while they were attending courses, by individuals already attending courses in care work and needing work placements. This removed the problem of cover for employers.)

Accused of encroaching on another provider's or organisation's territory? Best to call a meeting and clear the air as soon as possible. Are there any ways of collaborating so that you are not duplicating activities? What can you all bring to the party? Can your organisation make a different contribution that will complement rather than compete with their work?

Feeling isolated? See if you can arrange to network and meet regularly with other outreach workers employed by your organisation or by other providers working in the same areas. Ask your manager(s) to allow time for you to engage in such meetings.

Experiencing a conflict of values between those of the institution and those of the constituency you are working with? Ask for a meeting with your manager(s) and explain that there is an incompatibility that may make it difficult to achieve anything sustainable. Reconciling such differences should not be your responsibility alone and may call into question the whole organisational purpose in doing outreach.

Difficult to get your employer to respond to some of the community learning needs that have been identified? Ditto. Ask to meet with senior managers and relevant heads of department and tutors. If there is resistance, write a report to senior managers outlining the difficulties and potential loss of credibility and requesting that they suggest a solution if they wish your work to be effective.

In addition: is there a local information and guidance service to which you can refer people? Can you suggest suitable alternative learning opportunities?

Remind your employer that working with new learner groups can benefit not only them but also the institution: through working with different communities, education and training providers can significantly raise their local credibility and profile.

Glossary

Community regeneration is a process of helping particular neighbourhoods or communities that have suffered from poverty, de-industrialisation, unemployment and other blights to recover through new social, cultural, educational, civic and economic activities.

Evaluation strategies are measures taken to monitor the effectiveness of any actions taken or procedures followed to achieve specific objectives.

First-rung provision is learning provision, usually of an informal nature, provided in response to the requirements or interests of people returning to organised learning for the first time since leaving school.

Formula funding describes funding arrangements based on specific central criteria that are applied to state funded education provision.

Gatekeepers are individuals in close contact with certain groups and who, by virtue of this relationship and their authority over the groups in question, are able to exercise some control over access to them by other people. Examples include employers, managers (for example, of voluntary groups), health visitors, religious leaders, wardens (for example, of day centres, bail hostels and residential homes).

Learning ambassadors/learning champions are individuals who have usually engaged in organised learning themselves and who, either informally because of their own enthusiasm for learning, or more formally after a period of training, set out to inform others about the availability and advantages of learning opportunities.

Lifelong learning is a term for which there is no universally accepted definition but which implies a learning process that continues throughout life according to the needs of people at different stages of their life cycle. The term is currently used rather loosely in educational and policy documents and is now often used synonymously with longer-established terms such as adult education and adult and continuing education, although logically it should apply to all age groups and all life stages.

Local Strategic Partnerships are new overarching partnerships of local authorities and other local organisations that will prepare strategies to address the needs of communities.

Non-accredited learning provision is learning which is not assessed according to specific criteria leading to an internal or external certificate.

Progression routes are learning pathways people can take between different levels of learning or between different learning environments. These can be created by offering gradually more advanced levels of learning in the same subject/discipline or skill area, or by providing mechanisms that help people move between different learning sectors and institutions such as advice and guidance and different forms of learner and learning support.

Social inclusion is a process of trying to bring the groups mentioned below into a situation whereby they can access and take advantage of the educational, social and economic opportunities available to other groups.

Socially excluded is a term applied to groups or individuals who, by virtue of factors such as poverty, unemployment, age, race, family, social or residential circumstances, ill-health, disability, learning difficulties or lack of basic skills, do not enjoy all the social and economic advantages available to other groups in society.

Sustainability means, in this context, the extent to which any work and activities started can survive and continue beyond the original agreed or funded period.

Widening participation generally refers to a process of trying to attract to, and engage in, organised learning individuals or groups who normally resist, or whose circumstances inhibit, participation. It can involve a very wide range of activities depending on the purposes and preferences of the education provider or organisation.

Further reading

Aldridge F (1999) *Short and Sweet*, Leicester: NIACE

DfEE (1999) *Skills for neighbourhood renewal: local solutions*: the final report of the Policy Action Team on Skills

Greenwood M, Merton A and Taylor S (2000) A*n evaluation of non-schedule 2 pilot projects*, London: Learning and Skills Development Agency

Howard U (2001) *Stimulating demand for learning: an ideas paper on attracting new learners*, London: Learning and Skills Development Agency

McGivney V (1999) *Informal learning in the community: a trigger for change and development*, Leicester: NIACE

McGivney V (2000[a]) *Recovering outreach: concepts, issues and practices*, Leicester: NIACE

McGivney V (2000[b]) *Working with excluded groups: guidelines on good practice for providers and policy makers in working with groups under-represented in adult learning*, NIACE/Oxfordshire Strategic Partnership.

Organisation for Economic Co-operation and Development (1999) *Overcoming exclusion through adult learning*, Paris: OECD

Taubman D (2000) *Aylesbury revisited: outreach in the 1980s*, Leicester: NIACE

Thompson J (2000) *Rerooting lifelong learning, resourcing neighbourhood renewal*, Leicester: NIACE

Watson A and Tyers C (1998) *Demonstration outreach projects: identification of good practice*, Final Report, National overview with individual project reports, DFEE/ SWA Consulting.

WEA (1999) *Best practice: effective teaching and learning in WEA courses and projects*, London, National Association.

Wood A (1999) *Oxfordshire County Council Lifelong Learning Outreach Strategy*, Oxfordshire County Council, October.

Wood A (2000) *A guide to outreach with laptops*, Leicester: NIACE